Affiliate Marketing

101 Great Tips and Ideas Proven to Kick-Start Your Affiliate Marketing

By Meir Liraz

Published by Liraz Publishing

www.BizMove.com

Copyright © Liraz Publishing. All rights reserved.

ISBN: 9781698298399

Table of Contents

1. The Single Most Critical Factor in Making Money Online — 5
2. 101 Tips and Ideas Proven to Kick-Start Your Affiliate Marketing — 9

Special Bonus: The Simple Strategy That Made Me an Internet Millionaire

3. The First Step: Discovering Profit-Driving Keywords — 27
4. The Second Step: Monetizing Your Site — 33
5. The Third Step: Creating a Site That Will Attract Tremendous Amounts of Traffic — 38
6. The Fourth step; Creating an External Linking Structure That Will Blast Your Site to the Top of Google — 44

Appendix 1: The 50 Best Paying Affiliate Marketing Markets — 55

Appendix 2: Sources for Backlinks Sorted by Category and Page Rank — 57

MEIR LIRAZ

1. The Single Most Critical Factor in Making Money Online

You may be wondering who am I and what qualify me to give you affiliate marketing advice. Well, my name is Meir Liraz. You may have stumbled on my name on the internet, probably in relation to my activities as a writer and publisher of business guides. This is just one side of me, the visible one. There has been another side to my online presence, a concealed one, as a leading player in the internet marketing arena.

I've been an active internet marketer since the first days of the Internet, back then the reigning search engines where dinosaurs bearing names like Alta-Vista, Infoseek and Lycos, while Google was just a vague idea in the minds of two brilliant Stanford University students.

As I don't believe in theories and opinions, I've tested dozens of Internet marketing ideas, strategies and variables. Some proved to be successful while others bombed (and served me well as learning experiences). I must've been doing something right as I managed to accumulate along the way a seven figure fortune. The bottom line is that I've come up with a simple strategy that has enabled me to make money online like crazy.

As a bonus, I've included within this book a special section where I describe exactly the simple strategy that made me an Internet Millionaire. This is a step by step guide that will allow you to mimic my method and make a killing online.

Why reveal my methods now? Well, I'm semi retired now and I've made enough money so that my kids do not have to work one more day in their lives (if they so desire). I've had my blessings and now I want to help others succeed as well, this is my way to give back.

Now look, 99% of the folks who try to make it on the Internet follow the same rout, the same set of activities. They all move in one big herd. Listen, In the highly competitive online arena, when you do the same things as anyone else you don't stand a chance to succeed - you are doomed.

In order to win the Internet marketing battles you must go off the beaten path, you need to do something different, you need a competitive edge - and that is where the simple strategy presented in the bonus section come into play. It will give you that "unfair advantage" to boost your sales, pile up profits and leave your competitors in the dust.

When a soldier goes into battle he seeks to equip himself with the best weapons he could lay his hands on. The same goes for the internet marketing battles. The single most important factor in utilizing this strategy successfully is equipping yourself with the right tools and services. The magic word is 'Automation'. You need to have the best tools and you need to know how to put them to best use. This is critical, some of the tools that I'll show you can actually heart you if not used correctly.

Look, in order to make money on the internet you need to get noticed by Google and you need to climb up the search engines' results pages (SERPs). Unfortunately Google gives preference to large and established sites. The little guy with a relatively new or small website does not stand a chance. You could of course go the "natural" rout. That will take you about 5 years to establish a site that will be liked by Google. I don't know about you, but I prefer to start making money with a new site much earlier than that. That is why you need to use some special tools, to take some unconventional measures - you need to be a little more creative. Sound complicated? don't worry, in the special bonus section, I'll give you exact instructions as of how to do it right.

Here's a list of the tools and services that I use while executing my strategy, later on I'll show you exactly how the strategy works and how these tools integrates perfectly within it to come up with the easiest, fastest, most effective way of making money online:

1. Keyword Research Tool: Keyword Canine - a multi-featured tool for niche discovery, keyword research and backlink analysis.

2. Hosting Service: HostGator - a reliable web hosting. Has some extra features that makes it suitable for internet marketing activities.

3. Wordpress Theme: Thesis - much more than a theme, it's more of a design and template manager for Wordpress. Most suitable for a business site that is meant to be ranked high on the search engines.

4. Content Creator: Article Builder - **produces high quality unique articles built around the topics and keywords that you give it.**

5. Email Marketing Tool: Weber - automatically manage all email marketing activities: creates sign-up forms, collects and manages subscribers, sends out scheduled emails and more. Powerful yet very easy to use.

6. Article Spinner: The Best spinner - a multi-featured tool for creating multiple versions of an article that will be seen as unique in the search engines.

7. Links Building knowledge: Link Building Course - a comprehensive link building learning framework that is constantly updated to reflect the most recent effective link building strategies.

8. Manual Link Building: Rank Crew - an affordable and reliable manual link building service.

9. Automatic Directory Submission: DeepLinkerPro - automate the creation of manual directory links, allows the use of varied anchor text and also to drip feed the submissions over time to make it all look as natural as possible.

10. Automatic Link Builder: Senuke - a powerful backlinking tool which has been designed to assist with the time consuming task of creating a large number of links.

11. Backlinks Indexer and Booster: Backlink Booster - automatically increases the power of the backlinks to a website. It's both a backlink indexer aiming to get the backlinks indexed faster, and also a backlink booster to help boost the amount of link juice each of the backlinks sends to a website.

Now, the next chapter features great tips and ideas **proven to kick-start your affiliate marketing**. Starting in chapter 3 I reveal the simple strategy that made me an internet millionaire.

2. 101 Great Tips and Ideas Proven to Kick-Start Your Affiliate Marketing

1. Create a short e-book and post it on document sharing sites. By doing this you can show off your expertise, but you can also attract visitors and prospective buyers who are looking for similar information, to your site . Be sure to include a number of links to your site inside the document.

2. When you try to make money through affiliate advertising, it is important that you stay up to date with all of the new trends and outlets to make money. Many affiliate advertising programs change, making it important that you stay on top of what is going on with the programs that are available.

3. Look into the payment structure of any affiliate program you are considering. Some offer a lifetime payout, while others offer a limited payout (such as per sale, or thirty to ninety days). Make sure that you are able to frequently check your balance to learn how much you are owed and how much has been paid out.

4. To maximize the money you make from your affiliate marketing program you need to make sure you are very open about your activities with advertising. People do not mind supporting blogs and forums that they enjoy or find useful but they also want to feel they can trust the person running it.

5. Let your affiliates help. If you have an affiliate program, let your affiliates do the promotion work for you. Offer them an incentive and they will be happy to do it. Your affiliates should have good-sized networks in place and when they publicize your articles, your website traffic will jump.

6. Be honest about the fact that you hope your visitors will help you out by clicking on your affiliate links. If it seems as if you are trying to hide the fact that you are an affiliate, your visitors will just go

straight to the vendor's website and purchase the product directly. Then you won't get credit; even though, you have put in a lot of work to promote the product!

7. A great affiliate marketing tip is to be aware of the regulations and rules that are set in place by the Federal Trade Commission. The Federal Trade Commission regulates advertisements and if you're caught breaking any of their rules, you might have to face the consequences and pay stiff fines.

8. There is a great chance that if an affiliate program is asking for a substantial bit of money down before you can begin the program, that they are going to get your money and never be heard from again. If they are requesting a good bit of money from the start, move on.

9. If you have affiliate ads on your website, you will get paid each time somebody buys a product by clicking on an ad. Do not trick people into clicking on an ad: this will not generate any income for you, and these people will never come back on your website or blog again.

10. Developing a healthy relationship with your affiliate is a great idea if you hope to be treated fairly. Look at it from the affiliate company's point of view. They're constantly running across people just trying to make quick buck. These guys tarnish their reputation with sleazy tactics. Be honest, supportive, and work to initiate conversations with people at the company.

11. Confirm how many sales the product really has before signing up with them. What is the point of spending your time building a site to promote a product that no one wants? You only get commission when someone buys so make sure you are putting your efforts towards a winner.

12. A great tip for all affiliate marketers is to understand the market in which they are advertising. Find potential problems in that

particular market as well as any limitations they might present, and do your best to work past them. You can find ample resources on the internet that will help you out.

13. All affiliate programs are different in what they offer and how payments are made. There is lifetime payout on sales on some programs, while others are on a 30-90 day structure. Also, some affiliates allow some flexibility on the types of ad units and colors and design to blend with your site better.

14. Learn as much as you can about marketing and sales. Business is always changing so you need to stay on top of new technologies and methods, and you have to do it before your competition does. Your affiliates benefit from everything you learn, so your education will go a long way toward building your business.

15. Give your readers a compelling reason to purchase the product you are promoting, right now. Do this by providing them with an action plan that involves using your product right away. Readers are tired of buying yet another product that sounds great but doesn't yet fit in their action plan. And they don't want to waste more cash on yet another info product. Give them a useful plan and they will see the value.

16. Write a short e-book about a topic related to the product or service your are marketing, include some of your affiliate links in it and upload it to some document sharing sites. This will attract new visitors to your links and also show potential buyers your expertise, making them more likely to trust your recommendations and buy products or services through your affiliate links.

17. If you have a website for your business, your domain name should be on everything that you own. Use your own personal vehicle, t-shirts, stationary, email signature and more, to constantly put the name of your website out there. Constant reminders will stick in people's heads and make them want to look it up.

18. Add content that your readers want along with your affiliate links. If you provide reasons for your audience to click on your links, you will find much better success. If you just type a list of baby items you like with links, you'll receive much less response than if you type reviews and why you loved these items.

19. Don't bother with products that don't convert, even if they advertise high commissions. One webmaster reported that out of over 1000 clickthroughs to a vendor's site, not one visitor actually bought the product. Terrible conversion ratios like this are a sign that the product is not in demand or that there is something wrong with the product, such as a high price or poor copy on the landing page.

20. It is important to know that with affiliate marketing, you are not required to make your own products. Instead, you be helping to sell another person's product. Knowing this is important because you can make just as money by selling someone else's product as you could if you were selling your own.

21. Use a redirect so that you can hide your affiliate link. Some customers will just take the domain name and remove the affiliate portion of the link in the hopes that they will get better pricing by "ordering direct". Using a redirect will force customers to actually use your link saving you your commissions.

22. Affiliate marketing can be summed up with two P's: patience and persistence. Not only do you have to plug away at various methods in order to effectively market your products, but you also have to be patient. If you think Rome took a long time to build, just imagine trying to create a successful business without a product. It takes drive and time to be an affiliate.

23. You must be willing to invest as much time and effort as possible if you are going to be successful with affiliate marketing. Look into training materials that are not overprices. Many times they will have the same information in them as the high-priced ones do. Save

yourself a couple dollars and gain the same amount of knowledge.

24. There is absolutely nothing wrong with asking an affiliate program for references! A good company will provide links to websites already making a profit off their partnership, but if they don't, ask! If they refuse to answer, or really don't know, then that is NOT a program you want to risk your reputation on.

25. Choose a niche market to sell to. Don't try to sell a different affiliate product to everyone. This dilutes your efforts and confuses your readers. Stay focused on products and services that serve customers in your specific niche. This will build up trust with your readers, increasing the chance that they will come back and buy your latest offerings.

26. In addition to checking out the product, make sure the company itself is legitimate and trustworthy. You will lose customers trust if you send them to a shady company that does not live up to its promises. Make sure that they follow through on their offers and that they handle their payments in a timely manner.

27. Remember that even a blogger who is doing it for fun can make money as an affiliate. If you have built up a following of people who read your site, consider working with an affiliate niche that fits your blog subject. Do not spam your loyal readers, but offer them something that you find useful as well and see the money roll in.

28. Record a short series of videos about the products that you are selling or topics that are in some way tied to those products. Be sure to keep the topics of your videos on subject to the products that you are selling so that the viewers will look at what you are promoting and purchase it.

29. In order for your affiliate program to be successful, it is imperative that you meet the needs of your reader. Why are they coming to your page? Is the information you are providing what they

are looking for? When you have your site designed properly, then decide what affiliate ads are relevant to the information you are providing your readers.

30. The way to analyze any potential affiliate marketing program is to weigh the potential returns versus the costs. It is important to go beyond simple dollars and cents in this analysis. A cheap affiliate program that requires tons of work from the webmaster is not as cheap as it appears. A profitable program that annoys and alienates website visitors may cost more business than it brings in.

31. If one affiliate program doesn't work for you, try another one. The various programs are not all the same. They offer different products, services, and payment. Some allow more freedom and flexibility, such as color and design, to help match your site better. Finally, you can even see if your favorite vendor or store has its own affiliate program. Mix and match until you find a program that fits your needs.

32. Who doesn't love a bit of free advertising? Get your business, and your website, listed in free business directories. There are many out there, such as Yelp, YellowPages.com, and InfoUSA. Listing with them can lead to a boost in website traffic as well as a boost in the success of your business.

33. If you find the website of the product owners not very well done, you can easily find affiliate link cloaker tools. These programs allow you to link any page from the company's website. Link your audience directly to the page where they can buy the product if your own website provides enough content.

34. Most importantly, your website content must be up to par. Your website will never get quality traffic if you are not targeting the consumer with information that is relevant and informative. An affiliate program will never work if you do not get good traffic directed through your site at a constant pace.

35. Offer visitors to your website exclusive content or services if they make a purchase from the advertisers in your affiliate marketing program. Do not restrict vital information this way, but make sure that visitors who do buy get something of definite value out of your websites bonus content. This will encourage both purchases from your affiliate and repeat visits to your website.

36. When you are pitching your product to a client, elaborate on what the product can do for them, instead of the actual design or functionality. Creating a more personal connection with the client can help them understand the value in putting money into your company, which will improve your business relationship.

37. Many people spend hours on the internet. They usually come across many advertisements per day, and will pay attention to the ones that are relevant to their lives. Putting an advertisement for your company on the internet is a sure way to make sure that hundreds of people will see it each and every day.

38. Developing and keeping a list of ideas handy is a great way to achieve in affiliate marketing. Once you learn a great tip or have one of those proverbial light bulb moments, always remember to make a note of it so you can refer to it later on. As you progress in your note-keeping, you can begin to form campaigns from loose ideas.

39. Join a two tier affiliate program that can provide you with a steady income source that doesn't require a lot of effort. In two tier plans, you make a small commission on every product that the affiliate underneath you makes which will generally net you a steady income stream.

40. Think positive. If you get involved with affiliate marketing and not expect it to work out well for you, you are likely to fail. Expect that you will be successful in this venture and you will find that with some information and some experience, you will make the money that you want to earn with time.

41. Always check the reputation of the companies you choose to do business with. You may hear stories about companies not paying the affiliate commission and getting by with it. You want to make sure you get what you are paying for and that's why it's best to check the company out before investing.

42. A great affiliate marketing tip is to post comments on popular YouTube videos that are relevant to your niche market. Posting comments on popular videos will get the attention of a lot of people. They'll also be able to check out your channel and see what else you have to offer.

43. If you have done your research and partnered into good affiliate marketing networks, you should take advantage of the marketing managers these networks employ. Your manager is an expert in affiliate marketing, and because you share profits with your partners, your manager has a vested interest in helping you make more sales.

44. Think about where you're placing your affiliate ads on your site, and change location if you don't think they're getting the kind of click-through you'd been expecting. This will help because people might ignore ads if they're at the right hand side of the page, but take notice if they're at the top. The best way to discover this is to experiment with the layout.

45. If you are not good at making and managing websites, opt for a blog. You can buy a domain name and associate it with your blog so that you still have a unique name. A blog is much easier to manage and you can easily create an attractive interface. You can also do some networking with other blog users.

46. The performance of an affiliate marketing arrangement can be boosted if the webmaster and the affiliate can agree to offer an exclusive product. A purchase that can only be made through an affiliate will be more tempting to a website owner's visitors, increasing click-through and earning more money for both the

AFFILIATE MARKETING

webmaster and the affiliate.

47. If you are working as an affiliate for a product or service that needs repeat business, keep this in mind during your promotions. Work up your marketing approach like you're fishing: The main goal is to throw out the bait and allow the fish to hook itself. After that, it's all about reeling in your catch.

48. Nothing seems to sell a product quite as well as scarcity. When a customer believes he or she only has a few minutes to get the product at the list price before the deal is no longer available, they're over three-times as likely to act. Use this technique in your affiliate marketing and make sure you instill a sense of urgency in customers.

49. A lot of successful affiliate marketers hold question-and-answer sessions with themselves in order to get ahead in the highly competitive marketplace. You should examine your market and then ask questions on how it could be improved. Of course, then you must work to provide the answers and to improve the market.

50, Use the internet to check the history of an affiliate program prior to signing on with them. It is so important to know who you are working with so you do not find yourself frustrated and angry about not getting the money that they owe you for selling their products.

51. A great tip for affiliate marketing is to start promoting an affiliate product on Facebook. Facebook is great because it allows you to get in touch with millions of other people. It can be a very powerful marketing tool and you'll definitely generate interest by promoting your product or service on there.

52. High pressure is not required! Remember that affiliate marketing is not the same as selling, so you really don't have to put yourself through a lot of stress to do it. You don't have to handle merchandise or inventory. You deal with prospects rather than customers. You only have to introduce your prospects to the product. You don't

really have to sell, so you are better off just being friendly and pleasant and making sure lots of people see the product.

53. Lifetime commissions, in affiliate marketing, are now quite rare. They should still be sought out since they could offer great rewards, though. When a referred customer buys something at the affiliate vendor's site, a commission goes to the person who referred them. In the majority of affiliate programs, that commission is paid only for the first purchase that the customer makes. They are definitely worth searching for.

54. Offering customers the option of joining an affiliate marketing program when they make a purchase will multiply sales! Think about every customer automatically promoting to other customers and you can see how quickly this profitable chain reaction could occur. It is quite possible that you will never need to pay for advertising again if you have your customers doing it for you.

55. Keep track of your affiliate program results. Successful affiliate sales come from watching what works and what doesn't. Most affiliate programs include some type of tracking function that helps you see which links are working well and which ones need to be tweaked. Vary page positions, see what products sell where, which wording helps links perform better, and use it to plan your future affiliate program strategies.

56. People looking for ways to make money in a hurry should avoid becoming an affiliate marketer. There are just no instant profits in a system like this. You must compete within your niche market and then drive traffic to someone else's product in hopes that they become a paying customer. There's nothing quick about that.

57. Something every affiliate marketer should understand is the importance of their websites layout. You want to pick a layout that adequately represents the image you want your page to portray. You should choose a style that matches the items you will be advertising.

Having a layout that looks good will keep people engaged in your site.

58. If you perform especially well for a particular company, ask for a raise. If you are generating enough sales, the marketing program you joined will be eager to keep you.

59. A great way to make sure that your site is interesting is to choose a topic that you like. If you are writing about a site and advertising for things that suit you, then it will be easier and more interesting. Advertising for what you love is the number one rule for affiliate marketing.

60. If you are ever going to make money in the affiliate marketing industry, it is important that you buy a domain name. While this may seem obvious, the novice may not know what affiliate advertising entails. You should try to get a domain name that fits your product perfectly.

61. To increase the success of your affiliate marketing, discover the type of tracking software a company uses before you join their affiliate program. If the program does not track all of your sales, then you will not receive credit for all of the viewers that you refer to their company.

62. Before you sign up with an affiliate service, you should make sure that the company you're choosing, offers real-time statistics. You will want to check your progress, to see if there are any changes you need to make to your campaign. This is very difficult to do if the site you're dealing with, does not update in real-time.

63. To increase profit, try to be as unique as possible when you are writing the text of your website. The more individualized you are the better chance that you have to stand out from the pack. This will result in an increase in sales and more credibility for your organization.

64. Make sure you know your audience when you build your affiliate program. Find out what their needs are and what age group they belong to. Build your site to provide a solution to your visitors. The main theme of your site should match the products of your retailer. Don't place unrelated links on your site just because they pay well.

65. Always keep in mind that the quality of the affiliate products you promote on your website can very much affect your reputation. If you go for the best, readers will sing your praises to all levels of the internet. If you choose badly, those same folks will drag your reputation into the mud, giving you worse-than-zero credibility.

66. Look for an affiliate program that offers a high commission. This way you will make more money than dealing with a program that pays out less commission. Companies that offer a higher commission usually know what they are doing and have been in the business long enough to offer a higher commission for you.

67. Do not make the mistake of focusing on just one sales technique. You might have the best blog in the world, but you are still losing out on customers who need a little more push or don't like reading a blog. Advertise on other sites. Send out emails with value added sales techniques to take people from prospects to customers.

68. Before adding an affiliate product to your business, test it first. It's very difficult to recommend a product to your customers if you have no personal experience with the product. Get the product yourself, contact people who have purchased the product before and read up on online reviews from actual users. It will pay off in the long run, as you will be able to market the product more effectively.

69. A great tip for every affiliate marketer is to incorporate in their site a plug-in module or portal that rotates through ads. This is a great way to get new ads on your site and it allows you to swap out the ads that are not making you any money and leave the ones that generate adequately.

70. Don't have a TV in your home office! It's a huge distraction which can lead to making mistakes if you end up paying more attention to it than the work you're doing. If you must have a television turn it off during work hours, and keep focused on what you're doing to better your affiliate marketing strategies.

71. Beginner affiliate marketers often make rookie mistakes because they did not do proper research. One of the biggest mistakes is overloading your page with banners. Too many banners lower your traffic and lose your affiliate commissions. Too many banners also may slow down your page load time.

72. There has been endless debate on which is the best format for a sales page. A good alternative is to insert 'more detail' links throughout the body of the short copy and have them come up as pop ups which the reader can open and close while remaining on the main page.

73. When it's time to redesign your web site, you might have questions as to how. Maybe it's time for you to ask the question 'What is the real purpose of my site?' and redesign it accordingly. If you focus on your site's purpose and its niche on the web, then you will be able to create a much more user friendly design.

74. Many affiliate marketers do themselves a disservice by straining too hard to turn into "super" affiliates. Generally speaking, they attempt to sell more products than they can effectively promote, and ended dropping the ball on all of them. Keep in mind that maximum results are not true. Give yourself plenty of time so you can develop a plan that works.

75. If you are reviewing a product that you have not purchased, make sure that you always include examples of how it works. You always want to give screen shots of the product, other reviews from users (with permission), and other vital information about the product. As an affiliate, you should be really informed about any product you

promote.

76. To market your business in a personal way, take advantage of streaming video. Sites like Youtube will host a video for you at no cost. Being able to see you talk about your products will draw customers to your site and let them feel like they know you. Because Youtube has a high page ranking, this is also an excellent way to get more search engine traffic.

77. Be sure to sign up for more than one affiliate program. In this way you will protect your income, and be able to produce a more interesting website with more to offer. If you are offering more than one kind of product or service, you won't go under if one company changes its policy or goes out of business. You will still have other sources of income to rely upon.

78. You should never allow slow earnings to deter you from becoming an affiliate. Sometimes, affiliates choose a product that they think is good but that is not so good at all. You might still get the traffic but fail to sell. If this is the case, your trafficking techniques are working; you just need to pick a better product.

79. If an item isn't selling on your website, reconsider where it is placed on the page. When trying to sell an item that you believe should be moving units, consider if it's in the wrong category or in an awkward location on the page. Check with keyword tools, to see if the item has a title and description that should be driving people to it and if not, fix it!

80. Have focus groups made up of your customers and visitors review your site on a regular basis. The use of a focus group will allow you to really find what customers think of your products and the way you are presenting them. You may also get new ideas that will help you increase your profits.

81. Learn about search engine optimization before you start building

your site. There are a lot of pitfalls in SEO that you don't want to end up falling into. Learn what type of keywords work for your site and the best ways to utilize them in order to increase your rankings. The more people who can find your site, the better you will do.

82. The best affiliate marketers out there are innovative marketers. Relying only on the tips and tricks you read throughout various web articles will only get you so far. And that's because everyone's doing the same thing. You should soak up the information and use solid advice to build your own unique strategy.

83. Developing a healthy relationship with your affiliate is a great idea if you hope to be treated fairly. Look at it from the affiliate company's point of view. They're constantly running across people just trying to make quick buck. These guys tarnish their reputation with sleazy tactics. Be honest, supportive, and work to initiate conversations with people at the company.

84. Understand that you are going to have to put time into your site. A lot of people are dazzled by the idea of making a thousand dollars a week without doing any work. That is possible, but not until you have built your site and reputation up to the point where you don't have to do much. Getting to that level requires significant time investments and if you aren't ready to put in the time, this may not be the business for you.

85. Make sure you pick products that you are familiar and comfortable with. You want to pick something that you know you can advertise well to maximize the amount of potential profit available to you. You don't want to get stuck trying to promote products you have little or no information about.

86. A great way you can appear to be trustworthy to your audience in article marketing is to use testimonials on your site or within your articles. Testimonials from real users show that the product or service you're marketing is actually effective and can help people for the

better if they only purchase the product.

87. Test out the affiliate programs customer service by putting in a service ticket or calling about a problem. Pay attention to how you are treated and if they are able to solve your issues. Nothing throws a customer off like bad customer service. If you have sent someone to a product and they have a bad experience, you will be linked to that bad experience in their eyes. Avoid companies that can't deliver a good experience to your customers.

88. Try out different affiliate programs until you find ones you like. Choose different services, payment structures and products. Some pay you residuals forever, while others only pay for one to three months. Some affiliate programs will give you more choices for ad units, letting you change designs and colors to customize them to your site.

89. Once you understand the basics of affiliate marketing, begin networking with other marketers. By making solid industry connections, you can set up joint ventures to help each other succeed. Try attending affiliate marketing conferences to connect with other marketers and merchants in person. The relationships you build can lead to long term success in the industry.

90. A great way to increase your profits from affiliate marketing is to incorporate your marketing program into your email communications. If you have faithful customers you can include a link to your affiliate's products in your newsletters or special offers. This will create more exposure to your affiliate link which will result in a profit gain for you.

91. Track and analyze the exact source of every visitor to your affiliate links. By doing this you can identify which marketing techniques are bringing in visitors and, more importantly, where visitors with the highest conversion rates originate. You can then concentrate your time and money on only the successful marketing

AFFILIATE MARKETING

techniques.

92. To maximize the money you make from your affiliate marketing program make sure that you present your information cleanly. You want to focus on the content and the advertising, not distracting your readers with other items to focus on. Ask yourself if you need each component and get rid of the ones that do not make you money.

93. Establishing a legitimate business should be your ultimate goal over simply selling a product. Practically anyone can sell a product online, if they're offering the right type of product and are getting it noticed. But, it takes a skilled businessperson to actually build a brand name and experience long-term success.

94. Affiliate marketers should be attacking the mid-sized markets in this current type of economy. You won't be able to do well in a low market, and you won't be noticed in a high market. If you can achieve in the middle, however, you'll stand out like a varsity-level athlete playing freshman football.

95. You'll need to consider affiliate marketing a full-time job to really profit enough from it to live off the income. That means dedicating yourself to updating your website with fresh content, swapping out graphics and links, seeking new tools to better your strategies, and keeping track of statistics and accounting.

96. Affiliate marketing requires a lot more than selling great products; it also requires you keeping an up to date site to work as your digital shop. Use current web layouts or news on your domain to keep the patron's attention. If you let your design or products run out of date, you will notice that you can't bring in those same quality customers you could previously.

97. Before picking an affiliate marketing partner, you should visit their website to get a feel for their online business. Would you personally buy from their website? Is their website easy to use?

Would visitors to your website feel good or bad about being directed to the advertiser? You can learn plenty about potential partners just by checking their site.

98. Many companies that deal in affiliate marketing want you to have an established website or blog before they allow you to link to them. This will mean that you will need to have many posts, good content, high search engine rankings, and a large following. Then you will be able to link to several companies as an affiliate.

99. Nothing is quite as important in affiliate marketing as correctly identifying your audience. Understanding that there are different niche markets within every niche market will help you to only target those potential customers most likely to purchase a product. This saves you a lot of time and helps you make a lot more money.

100. To increase the success of your affiliate marketing, work on adding to your passive income through programs that offer continuity. Successful marketers have various continuity programs that offer reoccurring income over an extended period of time. This reoccurring income will provide a sound financial base that you can then build upon.

101. If you are attempting to market multiple products after the success of your first campaign in affiliate marketing, you should try to keep the product in relatively the same market. You already know how to promote a product within this market. So remember this analogy: Don't go from fixing cars to fixing airplanes.

Special Bonus: The Simple Strategy That Made Me an Internet Millionaire

3. The First Step: Discovering Profit-Driving Keywords

There is a special breed of Online-Millionaires that are making money on the internet like crazy. You've probably never heard of them. They keep themselves and their activities under the radar. Why? because they follow a certain simple strategy and they don't want you or anyone else to discover it. This strategy has created more millionaires than you could ever think possible.

How do I know? I am one of those Millionaires, and I'm going to reveal to you now each and every component of this incredible strategy.

My name is Meir Liraz. You may have stumbled on my name on the internet, probably in relation to my capacity as a writer and publisher of business guides. This is just one side of me, the visible one. There has been another side to my online presence, a concealed one. And there is where I've been taking advantage of that simple strategy to accumulate my seven figure fortune.

So why reveal my methods now? Well, I'm semi retired and I've made enough money so that my kids do not need to work one more day in their lives (if they so desire). I've had my blessings and now I want to help others succeed as well, this is my way to give back.

Now look, 99% of the folks who try to make it on the Internet follow the same rout, the same set of activities. They all move in one big herd. Listen, In the highly competitive online arena, when you do the same things as anyone else you don't stand a chance to succeed - you are doomed.

In order to win the internet battles you must go off the beaten path, you need to do something different, you need a competitive edge -

and that is where my simple strategy comes into play. It gives you that "unfair advantage" to boost your sales, pile up profits and leave your competitors in the dust.

When a soldier goes into battle he seeks to equip himself with the best weapons he could lay his hands on. The same goes for the internet battles. The single most important factor in utilizing my strategy successfully is equipping yourself with the right tools and services. The magic word is 'Automation'. You need to have the best tools and you need to know how to put them to best use. This is critical, some of the tools that I'll show you can actually heart you if not used correctly.

Look, in order to make money on the internet you need to get noticed by the search engines and you need to climb up the search engines result pages (SERPs). Unfortunately Google and the other search engines give preference to large and established sites. The little guy with a relatively new or small website does not stand a chance. You could of course go the "natural" rout. That will take you about 5 years to establish a site that will be liked by Google. I don't know about you, but I prefer to start making money with a new site much earlier than that. That is why you need to use some special tools, to take some unconventional measures - you need to be a little more creative.

As a matter of fact, one of the best kept secrets of the cyber-millionaires is what tools they use and, more importantly, how they make use of them for maximum benefit.

Now I'm going to show you exactly how this simple strategy works and how the tools integrate perfectly within it to come up with the easiest, fastest, most effective way of making money online.

The way my strategy works is simple. You focus on creating quick little sites that each target a laser targeted long-tail keywords. Once you complete one site you quickly move onto the next. So you don't want to spend too much time on any one site. This way you create, one by one, an army of passive income websites that keep producing cash for years.

I'll show you exactly how to create and promote your first money making website, than you just rinse and repeat to create as many websites as you wish, the more sites you create the more money you make. The only limit is how far you want to go.

Now let's not waste any more time and move directly to the first component of the strategy which deals with deciding on the keywords your site is going to target. This is a crucial decision and a fundamental part of achieving success online. You could do everything else perfectly, but target the wrong keywords and your site will be a total failure. in this chapter I'll tell you exactly what to look for when searching for good solid keywords.

Most Internet Marketing "experts" and the self-proclaimed gurus will tell you to use the Google Keyword Tool (now called: "Keyword Planner" and is only available to Adwords account users) for your keyword research. This is a big mistake! if you only use the Google tool you'll end up going in circles with the rest of the herd achieving no success. Why? although the Google tool will provide you with a nice list of several hundred keyword variations, it will tell you nothing as to the competitiveness of the terms. You have no clue as to how hard it will be to rank in the search engines for any specific term. This is critical. Most newbies will choose a term from the Google Tool that is too competitive and end up hitting a brick wall. You certainly don't want to be spending any time or money building a site that will never rank in the SE's.

In order to implement the strategy successfully you need to utilize for your keyword research a tool named Keyword.

Keyword Canine (KC) will also provide you with a nice list of several hundred keyword variations but it goes beyond the Google Tool in that it will also analyze the competitiveness of each keyword variation. This is crucial and that is where you gain your "unfair advantage" over the 99% that only use the Google Tool.

How does KC do it? it has a special algorithm in its backend that looks at the top 10 Google search results for your chosen keyword and produces an accurate analysis in the form of "Very Easy, Easy, Moderate, Hard or Fierce" so you can literally plug in your keyword and get an instant answer.

Keyword Canine has a ton of additional features that can help you as an Internet marketer but for the purpose the implementation of my strategy, the competition analysis is what we need.

I'm not going to walk you here thru the steps of conducting a keyword research with Keyword Canine as they have pretty good tutorials explaining everything. Simply sign for the service and follow their instructions.

Now let's see what properties a keyword must have in order to make us the most money.

For starter it has to be of a commercial value. This relates to our business model, the way we monetize our site. I will elaborate on this in a later chapter but for now I can tell you that our income will come from two sources:

a. Google AdSense ads.

b. Affiliate Programs

To maximize our income from those two we need to look for keywords in markets that has AdSense advertisers and affiliate programs that are willing to pay us top dollars. in the appendix you can find a list of the 50 best paying affiliate marketing niches. These are the markets that has a high concentration of AdSense advertisers and affiliate programs that are willing to pay top Dollars for your referrals. If you plan to tap any of these niches you must take into consideration that these are also the most competitive ones. However, I think it is still possible to find gem keywords in these areas provided you do your keyword research right. Alternatively you can look at other, less competitive, niches and still make good money as long as you take into consideration their commercial value.

Another property that you want to consider when looking for good keywords is the search volume. Obviously, even a #1 ranking isn't going to do you any good at all if nobody searches for the keyword that you rank for. I would say that the minimum search volume you should look for is 500 monthly searches (Keyword Canine shows you the search volume right next to the keywords in the list). Some will say that this is too low to target, however I had many successes with pages targeting close to this number of monthly searches.

The next property you need to consider for a good keyword is how competitive it is, how hard it will be to have it ranked in the first page of Google's search results. This is critical, however if you use Keyword Canine it will do the competition analysis for you and come with a recommendation in the form of "Very Easy, Easy, Moderate, Hard or Fierce". I would not go beyond "easy" with a new site.

So to summarize, in order to find a good keyword you need to consider:

* Commercial value

* Search volume

* competition strength

How many keywords should you target in one site? Some will tell you that you need to look for several terms and optimize each page in the site for a different term. This is not how my strategy works. For the small niche sites that we create it is best to dedicate each site to only one keyword and direct all our Search Engine Optimization (SEO) efforts towards the main page that is optimized for that keyword. We don't want to dilute our efforts by targeting several keywords in a site. With this concept in mind we don't want to waste our time looking for other keywords that will not rank anyway. Your time is better spent working on your linking structure (discussed later) or researching new keywords for new sites.

4. The Second Step: Monetizing Your Site

The Simple Strategy's business model is based on 2 sources of income:

a. Google AdSense ads.

b. Affiliate Programs

Which is better? there is no clear answer to this question. Some niches will produce better with affiliate programs while others with AdSense, you should test on a niche by niche bases. Usually you'll make more money with an affiliate site, unfortunately there may be many instances where you will find a good niche with keywords that can be easily ranked but no suitable affiliate program, in this case you'll use AdSense ads, and by the way, this will happen to you a lot.

Once you find a good keyword to target you start looking for an affiliate program that will go with this site. As a rule of thumb you should always prefer to promote digital products (eBooks, software, online services, etc.) over physical products. Why? because digital products come with higher margins which in most cases translate into higher commissions to the site owner.

Where can you find good affiliate programs to promote?

Your first bet should be the Clickbank Marketplace.

Clickbank offers thousands of products, look for products that are 100% relevant to your niche and has a credible sales page.

If you can't find a suitable product at Clickbank try one of the following affiliate program directories:

Commission Junction **(http://www.cj.com)**

Affiliatetips.com (http://www.affiliatetips.com)

AssociatePrograms.com

(http://www.associateprograms.com/directory/)

Affiliatesdirectory.com (http://affiliatesdirectory.com/directory)

If you still can't find a suitable affiliate program try a Google search that combines your keyword with the word "affiliates" and other similar variations. Sometimes this works and you will find one or more good affiliate offers for your niche.

If all of the above does not work and you can't find an affiliate program that is relevant to your target niche, monetize your site with AdSense ads. This is not necessarily a bad thing. I had AdSense ads that produced $5, $6 and even $9 per click.

Anyway, don't ever be tempted to post affiliate links that are not fully relevant to your target keywords! this will never produce satisfactory results.

Where should you place your affiliate links and AdSense ads on the page? The best spot would be right below the top article title and above the article body, if you are using Wordpress it would be directly below the post title and above the post content. This would be the spot that will by far produce the best results.

As for the AdSense ads, I always match the background and border of the ad with the background of the theme where the ad will be placed and I recommend you do the same - my tests show that this increases the effectiveness of the ads. You can use a plug-in for Firefox and Chrome called Colorzilla (http://www.colorzilla.com/) to help you do this quickly.

Another good option for the affiliate links is to embed them within the text, preferably towards the top part of the article.

As for affiliate links, my tests show that reviews and text ads will, in most cases, outperform banners. I guess some folks simply ignore banners altogether. I seldom use banners to promote affiliate offers,

AFFILIATE MARKETING

I've always found effective ways to present affiliate offers with text only. I will be the first to admit that my pages are not very pretty, but hey, I'm not in the business of creating cute pages, I am in the business of making money, and for this my "not pretty" pages are doing very well.

Below is an example of affiliate links embedded within an article:

> **Free Car Insurance Deals**
>
> Here's How to Get Free Car Insurance Deals
>
> So you are interested in locating free car insurance deals. Well, I will show you now not just how to find those free deals but rather how to find the cheapest car insurance rate that is available in your area.
>
> The single most critical factor in getting the best auto insurance deals is shopping around for as many quotes as you can. How many? you should go for at least 5 quotes from different auto insurance companies, less than that will simply not do the job.
>
> Now, the problem is that shopping around for five quotes can be a tedious and time consuming task - well, not anymore, now it can be much easier for you.
>
> We've reviewed numerous quoting services to bring you the best two. Each of the following free services can provide you with several competing quotes from various companies, thus enabling you to compare and pinpoint on the best rate that is available for your location. in order to maximize your chances of getting the best rate possible we recommend you use both services:
>
> InsurMe - May save you hundreds on your car insurance. Simply enter in your zip code and get free quotes from providers in your local area that offer great rates.
>
> Kanetix - Provides multiple company insurance rates, see how companies compete for your business. Offers great rates from quality insurers.

Here's is an example of affiliate links in a review format placed under the title of an article. By the way, I've used this format, "The 5 Best ...", multiple times with various niches. Over the years this format proved to be very profitable for me.

> ### Car Insurance Information Center
> ### 7 Day Car Insurance, Compare to Get Low Cost Rate
>
> **The 5 Best Car Insurance Quotes Providers**
> We've reviewed dozens of auto insurance companies, brokers and agents to bring you this elite list of brands with the best free quotes online and very cheap rates. We recommend you get a quote from each company so that you will be able to compare and get the best rate. This comparison will allow you to save as much as $500 and more on your vehicle insurance.
>
> 1. **Car Insurance Finders** - May save you hundreds on your car insurance. Simply enter in your zip code and get free quotes from providers in your local area that offer the best rates.
> 2. **USInsurance** - Simply fill out the quick form and this system will match you up with the cheapest offers in real-time. You get low cost custom tailored quotes within minutes.
> 3. **InsureMe** - Provides multiple company insurance rates, see how companies compete for your business. Offers great rates from quality insurers.
> 4. **2Insure4Less** - Provides comparison quotes which can be purchased immediately, offers great rates.
> 5. **Kanetix** - Offers one of the easiest to use, and most 'consumer-friendly' instant insurance comparison service available.
>
> For many people, it is not easy to get a large amount to cover something such as insurance coverage. It could be a significant wide range of dollars to cover at one time, therefore, the choice of no deposit car insurance is often rather appealing.
>
> No deposit car insurance implies that you get instant auto insurance protection straight away, when the insurance policy is put over your car, so you do not need to pay anything in advance. You are able to pay the insurance policy on a monthly base in payments; nevertheless, you may have to offer a credit card for guarantee that you submit several

Build an Email List

The biggest sin committed by internet marketers is not building an email list made of emails collected from visitors and customers. In order to maximize the profit potential of your site you need to create an email list. Fortunately, all the aspects of building and maintaining a list can be, and should be, automated. Selling to your list is the easiest money you're going to make.

Now I'm not going to teach you basic Email marketing here, you'll find plenty of resources online. However, here are 4 important points that you should consider:

1. Build an opt-in form and integrate it into your home page. Place it "above the fold," so visitors can see it immediately and don't have to scroll down.

2. Offer a lead magnet, something that has value that you offer in

exchange for the visitor's email address. This could be a free eBook, a special report, a webinar, a list of tips, Etc. You have to tailor the offer to fit your niche so that you keep your list targeted, this is important.

3. Use AWeber to manage your list building and marketing activities. Aweber is the industry standard. It's extremely powerful yet very easy to use, most of the successful internet marketers use it. Working with Aweber is a breath, it will automate all your email marketing activities: creating your sign-up forms, collecting and managing subscribers, sending out scheduled emails and more.

4. Email marketing is about creating a relation with your visitors and customers, it's about trust. Do not abuse it by spamming your list with frequent blatant sales offers. Send them at list 3 useful, content filled, emails for each email that contains a sales offer.

5. The Third Step: Creating a Site That Will Attract Tremendous Amounts of Traffic

Once you have chosen your keywords you are ready to build your site. For your domain name you should strive for an exact match domain (EMD) if available. So if your keyword is 'women car insurance' you'll go for www.womencarinsurance.com. if this is not available try the .net, .info or any other TLD that happens to be available.

EMD domains used to get you a big advantage with Google - but not anymore. Unfortunately Google has changed their algo regarding EMDs but it can still get you some extra points, and of course anything that Google gives we are willing to take.

As for the hosting service I highly recommend you use, They are reliable, responsible and very suitable for internet marketing activities.

The cheapest and fastest way to build an effective niche site is to use Wordpress. and by the way, HostGator is probably the easiest web hosting platform to install Wordpress on. Using a few clicks of the mouse, your HostGator-hosted Wordpress site will be up and ready in less than five minutes. look for instructions at their site.

Once Wordpress is installed on your server there are some modifications that you need to make to the site.

First you need to set Wordpress to present SEO Friendly Permalinks. Although we don't' concentrate on the internal pages of our site, they often can rank in the SE's. So it is very important to set a good URL structure. Once logged into Wordpress, Click "Settings" then "Permalinks" and change it from default to "Post Name." This will change the structure of the URL's from default (site.com/?p=114 for example) to a good, SEO friendly version (site.com/title-of-post-goes-here).

Now replace the default theme with another one, simply find a new theme that is simple and "clean" - use the automated theme installation process from within Wordpress.

"Appearance" then "Themes" (while logged into Wordpress) then click the "Install Themes" tab. Leave all of the fields empty (they are by default) and then click the "Find Themes" button.

Next, Clean the theme from unnecessary elements - by default, most themes have the sidebar loaded up with useless things like META links, a calendar, archives etc. The footer also typically contains one or more links that can be removed and there are a few other useless things included by default as well. So the next step is to clean all of that up! We don't want excessive external links draining the authority we generate, which could be going back into our internal pages. And we want everything focused on the content and the ads.

Now you need to set the homepage to show only one article - it needs to look more like a static site and less like a blog. Primarily because it reduces canonical URL's and duplicate content. To do this, you're going to publish the homepage article as a page rather than as a post!

Once you've done that, click "Settings" then "Reading" and select the "A static page" radio button and then next to "Front page" select the page that is optimize for your keyword and then click "Save Changes." Now view your site in a browser and you should see that article, and that article only, on the homepage.

Now Clean up the footer and the sidebar and remove any unneeded links like the link to the theme creator's website, the link to Wordpress, Etc.

What theme should you choose for your Wordpress site?

While there are many free Wordpress themes out there, I recommend you use a theme called Thesis (If the link doesn't work, copy and paste the following URL into a browser:

http://www.liraz.com/thesis). This is much more than a theme, it's more of a design and template manager for Wordpress and it's the best theme for a business site that is meant to be ranked high on the search engines.

Now what about content?

You need to start with at list 6 article pages for a new site. Each article should be 500 to 1000 words long.

The best source for site content is a service called Article Builder.

Article Builder produces high quality unique articles built around the topics and keywords that you give it. Each article is built by weaving together snippets to build an article based on your category and subtopic choices. They have tens of thousands of categorized snippets in the database, every time you generate an article, it's different!

If article builder does not have articles in your topic you'll have to contract someone to write the articles for you, this is not expensive. Simply run a Google search for "article writing" or "articles writers" and you'll get plenty of offers.

In addition to being a good source of content Article Builder has another extremely useful feature. It can post content automatically to your Wordpress site on the schedule you choose. Why this is important? because Google likes sites that are being updated with new material on a regular basis. It is recommended that you set Article Builder to post a new article to your site once a week or about 3 articles monthly, this way you'll gain some extra points with Google.

Now here is a trick to creating articles fast and cheap. This is not very ethical and I am a bit shame telling you I did it, but anyway since I pledged to tell you all my tricks (or at least most of them ;-), I fill obliged to tell you about this one too, just that you'll know that this is available.

Here's how it works, you run a Google search with your topic as the search term, you add the word 'tips' or 'Guide' to the search. Now you collect several snippets from different good on topic articles that came in the search. next, you combine these snippets into one article. Now you spin this article with a spinner software to get an entirely new article. Just make sure you use the manual spinning mode so that your article will make sense.

In case you are not familiar with the concept of "spinning articles" here are some explanations. With this process you utilize a simple software program that takes an original article and alter it using replacement words (synonyms via an automated thesaurus) in order to create entirely new articles without having to re-write them. It's called "spinning" an article. This have many uses in the Internet Marketing field and we will talk about it later when we discuss linking strategies.

The best spinner software on the market today is called... The Best spinner. If you wish to be a successful internet marketer you need to familiarize yourself with this concept. They have on their site a nice video explaining its uses. You should take a look.

Optimizing Your Site For the Search Engines

Once you have your pages and content in place it's time to optimize them so that your pages will rank as higher as possible on Google and the other search engines. In this section we'll deal with the "On Page" optimization.

While the "Off-Page" optimization, mainly the external linking structure (that we'll discuses later), is what will give you your unfair advantage - the on-page optimization is a pre-requisite for the off-page to succeed. What I mean to say is that if the on-page optimization is not done right, the best off-line optimization in the world will not help you one bit. so you need to pay attention here.

I'll walk you now step by step in what you need to do:

1. Title tag - this is an HTML tag that goes within the header section of the page. Title tags are the most important on-page factor for SEO. Your keyword should be included within the title tag preferably close to the beginning of it. This is what Google shows on its search results page so you should also make it attractive so that it will entice searchers to click on it. Don't just throw your keyword there, make sure that it is appealing.

2. Headline tags (H1, H2, H3) - make sure your page include one H1 tag with your keyword in it. This headline tag shows Google that the text within it is important to the intended audience.

3. Meta Description tag - while this does not have a bearing on the ranking of the page, Google still pulls the text of how it describes your page to other people from this tag - be sure to make it attractive so that more people will be clicking your page.

4. Images - you should include at list 2 images in each page. Also add one video to one of the pages in your site, you can simply embed a video from YouTube. Make sure one of the images has your keyword in its ALT tag. All other images need to also have ALT tags but should not include your keyword in them. Too many ALT tags with your keyword can lead to an over optimization penalty by Google.

4. Keyword density - the exact keyword density is not important, I'll say it again, the exact percentage of the keyword density is not import. Simply include about 3 instances of your keyword in each page, one of them should be close to the beginning of the article, one of them can be in Bold or Italics and that will do (do not be tempted to overdo it - that's a common newbie mistake).

5. Synonyms - you can include 2 or 3 synonyms to your page that does not include exact words from your keyword.

6. Article Topic - this is important- your content should be on topic and match the niche and the keyword that is being targeted.

7. Outbound link - add one outbound link pointing to an authority site in your topic. This could be a Wikipedia page in a similar topic to yours. Place it at the bottom of the page, you can call it 'recommended source' or something similar. Ah, and do not add a 'no follow' tag to it, leave it in a natural state.

8. Unique Content - the page should be unique and not a duplicated one, if you are using a spun article it should be at least 75% unique. it should also be making sense and has decent grammar.

9. Length of articles - each page should be between 500 and 1000 words long. Be sure to vary the length of the articles in a site. Don't make all the articles exactly the same size.

Once your site is online and the on-page optimization is set, it's time to start creating links pointing to it. That's the subject of our next chapter.

6. The Fourth Step; Creating an External Linking Structure That Will Blast Your Site to the Top of Google

Search rankings for a specific keyword are primarily driven by the backlinks to your website using that keyword in the anchor text. But not all backlinks are treated equally. The more powerful a back link is, the more "juice" it flows into your website. And the more "link juice" that flows into your website, the higher your website ranks in search results. So both quantity and quality of back links are important in ranking higher in search results.

Getting external links, the link building phase of the Amazing Formula is the single most critical factor for attaining high rankings and consequently making money online.

Your link building activities are what will make or break your online business. On one hand, when done right, it can blast your pages to the top of Google - on the other hand, even a small mistake can drop your pages into the Google abyss.

Too many links containing the exact same anchor text - Boom, Busted!

Too many links from low quality sites - Boom, Busted!

Too many links coming from just one genre (e.g. only from directories) - Boom, Busted!

Too many links coming from non relevant pages - Boom, Busted!

You get the picture...

That is why I strongly encourage you to acquire every piece of link building knowledge you can lay your hands on. Sorry pal, there is no way around it. if you wish to succeed in internet marketing you must know link building. Even if you are planning to outsource your link building tasks, you should be able to supervise everything that is done for you, and you should ask that they get your approval in advance for all the details of each linking campaign they run for you.

Listen to what happened to me once...

One of my sites had a page that was ranked #6 on the first page of Google's search results for a very competitive term for a couple of years. This page was earning me a nice sum of money day in and day out. One day I decided to try to improve its ranking, I contracted a firm from the Philippines to do a small manual linking campaign for this page. This firm came highly appraised on the forums and the people there were nice and seem knowledgeable. At that time I was busy with a big project and also a bit out of laziness I neglected to ask for a preapproval. To make a long story short, one month and 400 Dollars later my page sank to the fourth page of the Google SERPs.

Now there are two morals to the story:

First, don't count on anyone to do a link building job for you without your approval, in advance, of any small detail of it.

Second, If you have a money producing page ranked anywhere on the first page of Google - don't mess with it!

If you are curious as to what went wrong with this campaign. In the postmortem I discovered that they created too many backlinks with the exact keyword as the link text - and this is something that Google does not like.

Now, the best link building knowledge source that I know of is the Link Building Course (If the link doesn't work, copy and paste the following URL into a browser: **www.liraz.com/linkbuilding**). I strongly encourage you to buy their course. It's a bit pricy but it is well worth the price. Look at it this way, each mistake that is not being avoided due to lack of knowledge can cost you many many times more than the price of this course.

OK, now we are ready to delve into the Amazing Formula's linking strategies.

For our external linking structure we are going to utilize the most effective most powerful linking strategy there is, called "Tiered Linking".

With Tiered Linking you build 3 tiers of links, the links in tier 1 points to your money page, tier 2 points to tier 1 and tier 3 points to tier 2. Basically you are building backlinks to your backlinks. This structure gives your first tier of backlinks more strength and authority. Over time your tier 1 backlinks will gain page rank and that link juice gets passed directly onto your site. It creates a knock on effect passing huge volumes of link juice and authority all the way down the chain to your site. Another advantage of this structure is that it gives search engine spiders thousands of paths and opportunities to land on your site which will further increase rankings.

Here's a diagram that gives you a representation of the Tiered Linking structure:

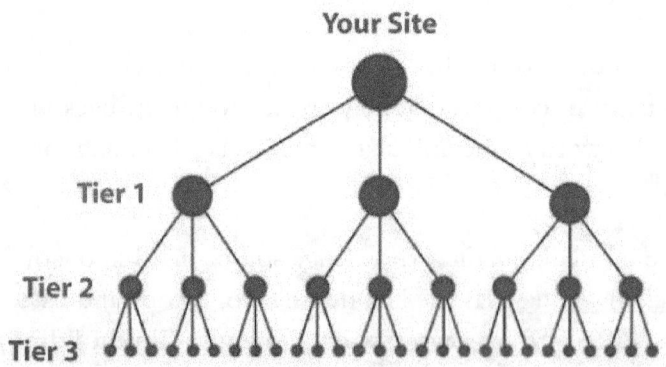

Now let's start with the process of building links for tier 1, these links point directly to your money site.

The links for tier 1 should be created manually and gradually. This means it should be done by you or outsourced to a firm that does manual linking - no automatic software at this phase. It should be spread gradually over two months, faster than that can trigger Google's penalty algos. You can't speed up stuff like building tier 1 links, or else you're going to get penalized.

If you don't have the time or the inclination to do the manual link building yourself, you can outsource it. This is what I'm doing. Manual link building is a tedious task so I usually hire someone else to do it for me. A good and reliable manual link building service that you can hire is Rank Crew (If the link doesn't work, copy and paste the following URL into a browser: **www.liraz.com/rankcrew**). I highly recommend them.

While building tier 1 you need to vary the anchor text as much as possible since Google discount too many instances of exact match anchor text. Follow these guidelines for the link text (anchor text) of your back links:

20% Main keyword exact match (e.g.: "main keyword")

20% Variation of main keyword (e.g.: "best main keyword resource")

50% Generic anchor text (e.g.: "click here, here, clicking here, good resource, see this, have a look")

10% URL of the page as the link text (e.g.: "www.mainkeword.com" or "mainkeword.com" or "http//:www.mainkeword.com")

Now to the actual link building. I can't teach you here all the aspects of doing basic linking, this is beyond the scope of this guide. You should be able to find plenty of resources for that online, or better off, buy the Link Building Course, this is the best resource of linking knowledge that I know of.

I will however give you some basic guidelines, point you to the right directions and provide you with a list of sites that can feature links pointing to your site.

Important Note: before you create backlinks with any site, make sure they are not adding the NoFollow tag to their links - do not create tier 1 links with sites that NoFollow their links.

Now here's a list of site's categories where you should build links for your tier 1 (find more sites in the Appendix):

Web 2.0's - great for creating mini sites with articles and videos that link back to your main site. You can use spun articles for the content. Here's where The Best spinner will come handy. You can use articles that are spun to 50%. Create 10 blogs here and post to them with your link embedded. Make sure the topics are relevant to your keywords, this is important.

Here's a sample of sites in this category (find more in the appendix):
wordpress.com
blogger.com
issuu.com
yola.com
tumblr.com
weebly.com
my.opera.com
livejournal.com
typepad.com
sfgate.com

Social Bookmarking - get your site bookmarked! 30 bookmarks will do it.

Here's a sample of sites in this category (find more in the appendix):
connotea.org
delicious.com
digg.com
reddit.com

slashdot.org
stumbleupon.com
citeulike.org
chime.in
bibsonomy.org
blinklist.com

Directories - web directories are a great source for links - strive for about 40 quality directory links submissions. Seems tedious? there is an excellent tool that can help you with this task. It will make creating manual links from directories a breath. I strongly recommend that you use it: DeepLinkerPro (If the link doesn't work, copy and paste the following URL into a browser: **www.liraz.com/deeplinker**) It allows you to use varied anchor text and also to drip feed the submissions over time to make it all look as natural as possible.

Here's a sample of sites in this category (find more in the appendix):
wordpress.org/showcase
abc-directory.com
cssdrive.com
cuedirectory.com
dirbull.com
dirnext.com
Elecdir.com
elsf.org
envirolink.org
freeprwebdirectory.com

Blog Directories - If you have a blog get it listed on these sites.

Here's a sample of sites in this category (find more in the appendix):
technorati.com
alltop.com
blogs.com
globeofblogs.com
blogcatalog.com

topix.net/dir
blogtopsites.com
blogtoplist.com
ontoplist.com
hotvsnot.com

Quality Article Directories - You can use spun articles for submission to these directories. Note that the better directories will review your articles before accepting to their site, so make sure they are grammatically correct and make sense. Submit to 30 directories here.

Here's a sample of sites in this category (find more in the appendix):
TheFreeLibrary.com
Ezinearticles.com
GoArticles.com
SelfGrowth.com
Gather.com
ArticlesBase.com
ArticleDashboard.com
ArticleSnatch.com
ArticleCity.com
Isnare.com

Video - create some videos and submit to video sites. You can find at fiverr.com folks that will create a nice video for you for 5 bucks a piece. 3 or 4 video submissions will do for this category.

Here's a sample of sites in this category (find more in the appendix):
youtube.com
vimeo.com
dailymotion.com
metacafe.com
truveo.com
videoegg.com
videobomb.com

veoh.com
liveleak.com
ifilm.com

RSS Directories - Create a RSS feed and submit to these sites. Submit to 30 directories here.

Here's a sample of sites in this category (find more in the appendix):
topix.net
blogdigger.com
feedage.com
feedcat.net
finance-investing.com
jordomedia.com
medworm.com
redtram.com
rssmountain.com
swoogle.umbc.edu

Doc Sharing - Submit a PDF file or a PowerPoint presentation here.

Here's a sample of sites in this category (find more in the appendix):
issuu.com
slideshare.net
scribd.com
docstoc.com
thinkfree.com
keepandshare.com
memoware.com
yudu.com
ziddu.com
docs.zoho.com

Press Releases - a good source for backlinks and news coverage - most of them cost money though.

Here's a sample of sites in this category (find more in the appendix):
businesswire.com
prlog.org
betanews.com
i-newswire.com
pitchengine.com
pr-inside.com
prlog.org
businessportal24.com
cgidir.com
free-press-release.com
information-online.com

Blog Guest Posting - guest blogging is a powerful link building strategy, however, it's a time-consuming pain in the butt! This can boost your rankings but it is not mandatory to the Amazing Formula.

Link Favors - ask friends, Acquaintances and family to place links pointing from their sites to yours.

Creating links for tier 2 and tier 3

Once you have all your tier 1 links set it is time to start building your tier 2 and tier 3 links.

While with tier 1 we were careful to create our links manually in order for them to appear as "naturally" as possible, with tiers 2 and 3 we can let the quality slip a bit and increase the overall quantity of links that we build.

We still want our links to be contextual and relevant, but we can now use auto generated content on a second tier without a problem. We can worry a lot less about the overall authority and page rank of the domains we are building links from as we start to move the focus away from quality and towards quantity.

For tiers 2 and 3 we are going to leave the "manual" path and move to the "automatic" path. We are going to use a tool that will generate all our tiers 2 and 3 automatically. The best tool for this task is Senuke (If the link doesn't work, copy and paste the following URL into a browser: www.liraz.com/senuke). This is the tool that most successful Internet marketers use.

Senuke is a very powerful backlinking tool which has been designed to assist with the time consuming task of creating a large number of links. I'm not going to describe here how Senuke works as they have videos on their site that describe it better than me. What I can tell you is that with Senuke you can create tired link structures. As much as Senuke is powerful it is very easy to operate, creating tiered links is as easy as moving images on a screen - you need to see it to believe, just go to their site and watch the video. Now, what you do with Senuke is create a 2 tiered structure. It looks like a pyramid - one tier points to another tire that points to one of your tier 1 links - you need to build a different structure for each of your tier 1 links. Use their schedule feature to spread it over time.

Some say that it is safe to also use Senuke for creating the tier 1 links. They may be right, however being the cautious guy that I am, I am not yet ready to test this Hypothesis. I would stick with using only manual methods for the tier 1 links and I strongly advise you to do the same..

In addition to Senuke The Amazing Formula calls for the use of yet another powerful tool called Backlink Booster (If the link doesn't work, copy and paste the following URL into a browser: **www.liraz.com/backlinkbooster**). Backlink Booster automatically increases the power of the backlinks to your website. It's both a backlink indexer aiming to get your backlinks indexed faster, and also a backlink booster to help boost the amount of link juice each of your backlinks sends to your website (use it on your tier 1 backlinks).

Now, if we have Senuke why would we also need Backlink Booster? The fact is that many of the backlinks you are building are never found by Google thus seriously diminishing your linking efforts. What Backlink Booster does is it builds backlinks to your backlinks in a way that all of those backlinks that Google didn't find, are now found by Google. This not just help Google discover all of your backlinks, it also "boost" them so that now more link juice gets passed to your site thus the authority they all possess is multiplied, which flows through to your website! So the end result is more, stronger backlinks!

My tests show that operating Backlink Booster in addition to Senuke creates a strong synergetic effect that translates in a much better Google rankings. It's the one-two punch that will get you that elusive Unfair Advantage. Anyway, in order to rip the full power of the Amazing Formula you need to activate both Senuke and Backlink Booster.

This concludes The blueprint of my simple strategy for making money online. Once you completed to create tire 2 and 3 links with Senuke and have Backlink Booster do its thing, all you have to do is sit back and watch your site climb the search engines rankings and the money that is pouring into your bank account.

Here's To Your Success

Meir Liraz

# # # #

Appendix 1: The 50 Best Paying Affiliate Marketing Markets

The following are the best paying affiliate marketing markets:

Acne
Aging
Allergies
Anxiety
Arthritis
Asthma
Auto Insurance
Back Pain
Beauty
Cancer
Cats
Cosmetic Surgery
Credit Cards
Credit Repair
Debt Consolidation
Depression
Diabetes
Dogs
Email Marketing
Employment
Fitness
Forex
Hair Care
Hair Loss
Health Insurance
Home Improvement
Home Mortgages
Home Owner's Insurance
Home Security
Homeschooling
Insomnia

Internet Marketing
Life Insurance
Muscle Building
Network Marketing
Nutrition
Online casinos
Online Poker
Parenting
Payday Loans
Personal Bankruptcy
Personal Development
Personal Finance
Pregnancy
Quit Smoking
Real Estate
Skin Care
Snoring
Stock Market
Stress
Teeth Whitening
Travel
Web Hosting
Weddings
Weight Loss

Appendix 2: Sources for Backlinks Sorted by Category and Page Rank

This list include the following categories:

* Web 2.0's

* Bookmarks

* Directories

* Blog Directories

* Quality Article Directories

* Video

* RSS

* Doc Sharing

* Press Releases

Important Note: before you create backlinks with any of the sites on the following list make sure they are not adding the NoFollow tag to their links - do not create tier 1 links with sites that NoFollow their links.

Web 2.0's

Domain	PR
wordpress.com	9
blogger.com	9
issuu.com	9
yola.com	8

tumblr.com	8
weebly.com	8
my.opera.com	8
livejournal.com	8
typepad.com	8
sfgate.com	8
cerncourier.com	8
angelfire.com	7
tripod.com	7
jimdo.com	7
webnode.com	7
posterous.com	7
over-blog.com	7
webs.com	7
diigo.com	7
bravenet.com	7
newsvine.com	7
squidoo.com	7
jugem.jp	7

tripod.lycos.com	7
salon.com	7
goodreads.com	7
alternet.org	7
rediff.com	7
multiply.com	7
plinky.com	7
officelive.com	7
bravejournal.com	7
schuelerprofile.de	7
freewha.com	7
blog.co.uk	6
blogs.rediff.com	6
moonfruit.com	6
zimbio.com	6
fc2.com	6
flavors.me	6
wetpaint.com	6
hubpages.com	6

shutterfly.com	6
quizilla.teennick.com	6
webstarts.com	6
xanga.com	6
podbean.com	6
ucoz.com	6
purevolume.com	6
metafilter.com	6
dailystrength.org	6
democratandchronicle.com	6
wikia.com	6
gather.com	6
skyrock.com	6
carbonmade.com	6
en.netlog.com	6
cafemom.com	6
glogster.com	6
travelblog.org	6
jigsy.com	6

tribe.net	6
blog.de	6
travellerspoint.com	6
zooomr.com	6
piczo.com	6
jazztimes.com	6
dmusic.com	6
fotki.com	6
blogsome.com	6
freeblog.hu	6
twoday.net	6
areavoices.com	6
journalspace.com	6
diaryland.com	6
siteforum.com	6
blinkweb.com	5
doomby.com	5
blogbaker.com	5
http://blogetery.com	5

blogdrive.com	5
onsugar.com	5
opendiary.com	5
thoughts.com	5
ourmedia.org	5
snappages.com	5
spruz.com	5
soup.io	5
sosblog.com	5
dinstudio.com	5
terapad.com	5
webspawner.com	5
migente.com	5
jukeboxalive.com	5
flixya.com	5
ourstage.com	5
sosblogs.com	5
kaneva.com	5
weblogs.us	5

hazblog.com	5
ziki.com	5
pinkbike.com	5
yousaytoo.com	5
wayn.com	5
freehostia.com	5
simplesite.com	5
insanejournal.com	5
blogtext.org	5
myanimelist.net	5
webgarden.com	5
blog.hr	5
boulderweekly.com	5
madville.com	5
beep.com	5
springnote.com	5
zoomshare.com	5
scrapbook.com	5
realbuzz.com	5

ewebsite.com	5
fixya.com	5
350.com	5
blogdetik.com	5
quietwrite.com	5
ourstory.com	5
blogetery.com	5
blog.com.es	5
lifeyo.com	5
weblog.ro	5
postbit.com	5
mytripjournal.com	5
galtime.com	5
freeflux.net	5
blogs.ie	5
worldofminecraft.com	5
foss4lib.org	5
busythumbs.com	4
blogskinny.com	4

mywapblog.com	4
mylivepage.com	4
foodbuzz.com	4
wists.com	4
blurty.com	4
wallinside.com	4
vilago21.com	4
nexopia.com	4
bloghi.com	4
getjealous.com	4
lagbook.com	4
supernova.com	4
hpage.com	4
ohlog.com	4
quechup.com	4
inube.com	4
fotopages.com	4
kiwibox.com	4
upsaid.com	4

weddingwindow.com	4
nearlyweds.com	4
spi-blog.com	4
xomba.com	4
tblog.com	4
tabulas.com	4
2itb.com	4
mahiram.com	4
meemi.com	4
profileheaven.com	4
shoutpost.com	4
blogspot.com.au	4
ontheroad.to	4
blog.ca	4
visualsociety.com	4
nireblog.com	4
blogreaction.com	4
pnn.com	4
freeblogspot.org	4

blogeasy.com	4
blogstudio.com	4
bloggum.com	4
bloggerteam.com	4
wikyblog.com	4
freeblogit.com	4
iseekblog.com	4
free-conversant.com	4
singledad.com	4
typolis.net	4
wikipages.com	4
buzzherd.com	3
publr.com	3
bloguni.com	3
iamsport.org	3
incompany.com	3
bizeso.com	3
flippingpad.com	3
sweetcircles.com	3

myindospace.com	3
weblogplaza.com	3
spyuser.com	3
modwedding.com	3
fotolode.com	3
blogge.rs	3
wedshare.com	3
blogono.com	3
iblog.at	3
journalfen.net	3
metsbook.com	3
salsahook.com	3
getwed.com	3
schuelerchat.net	3
blogster.com	2
directorise.com	2
glbsocial.net	2
uwcblog.com	2
medicalmarijuanalisting.org	2

AFFILIATE MARKETING

siterun.eu	2
gonegothic.com	2
blogpico.com	2
evood.com	2
donkbook.com	2
jacso.hk	2
makinitmag.com	2
inlocaltv.com	1
cloodles.com	1
my.telegraph.co.uk	0
livelogcity.com	0
flukiest.com	0
nyc.net.au	0
yapperz.com	0
deinekollegen.de	0
wheretogetengaged.com	0
hipero.com	0
yolasite.com	0
blogspirit.com	0

blogion.com	0
mynewblog.com	0
20six.co.uk	0
myblogsite.com	0
qapacity.com	0
blogstream.com	0
petbam.com	0
jamrie.com	0
honmag.com	0
jamendo.net	0
blog2blog.nl	0
journalhub.com	0
netcipia.com	0
getjelous.com	0
lastbyte.com	0
kambase.com	0
englandbd.co.uk	0

Bookmarks

Domains	**PR**

connotea.org	8
delicious.com	8
digg.com	8
reddit.com	8
slashdot.org	8
stumbleupon.com	8
citeulike.org	8
chime.in	8
bibsonomy.org	7
blinklist.com	7
diigo.com	7
folkd.com	7
mister-wong.com	7
news.ycombinator.com	7
newsvine.com	7
bizsugar.com	6
jumptags.com	6
tagza.com	6
xmarks.com	6

kaboodle.com	6
tagza.com	6
amplify.com	5
dotnetkicks.com	5
fwisp.com	5
ikeepbookmarks.com	5
kirtsy.com	5
netvouz.com	5
stumpedia.com	5
buddymarks.com	5
clipclip.org	5
dropjack.com	5
linkagogo.com	5
wirefan.com	5
mylinkvault.com	4
oyax.com	4
bookmarktracker.com	4
chipmark.com	4
cloudytags.com	4

de.lirio.us	4
freelink.org	4
bmaccess.net	3
blogbookmark.com	3
rambhai.com	3
blurpalicious.com	0
pineapple.io	0
startaid.com	0

Directories

Domains	**PR**
wordpress.org/showcase	8
abc-directory.com	7
cssdrive.com	7
cuedirectory.com	7
dir.yahoo.com	7
dirbull.com	7
dirnext.com	7
Dmoz.org	7
Elecdir.com	7

elsf.org	7
envirolink.org	7
freeprwebdirectory.com	7
ilovelanguages.com	7
medranks.com	7
musicmoz.org	7
nutch.org	7
paleoportal.org	7
realtor.com	7
relapi.org	7
thomasnet.com	7
archivd.com	6
art.net	6
bestwebgallery.com	6
Botw.org	6
business.com	6
charitychoice.co.uk	6
cssbased.com	6
cssbeauty.com	6

csselite.com	6
cssheaven.com	6
cssmayo.com	6
dexigner.com/directory/	6
diolead.com	6
directory.ac	6
ehef-newdelhi.org	6
ezilon.com	6
familyfriendlysites.com	6
Fishlinkcentral.com	6
hotvsnot.com	6
intellisparx.org	6
jayde.com	6
jhucr.org	6
joeant.com	6
kahuki.com	6
kinderstart.com	6
mavensearch.com	6
mobileawesomeness.com	6

nzs.com	6
scrubtheweb.com	6
siteinspire.com	6
sitepromotiondirectory.com	6
smsweb.org	6
somuch.com	6
styleboost.com	6
sumodirectory.com	6
thebestdesigns.com	6
ukinternetdirectory.net	6
usacitylink.com	6
vrg.org/links/	6
webdesigners-directory.com	6
webdesignfinders.net	6
webdirectory.com	6
2yi.net	5
aaaagencysearch.com	5
abilogic.com	5
Alivedirectory.com	5

allensguide.com	5
allspiritual.com	5
amphotech.com	5
arakne-links.com	5
artchain.com	5
azoos.com	5
boliviaweb.com	5
britainbusinessdirectory.com	5
britishinformation.com	5
business-directory-uk.co.uk	5
busybits.com	5
canadaone.com/business/	5
canlinks.net	5
capterra.com/browse	5
comeonaussie.com	5
creattica.com	5
css-showcase.com	5
cssleak.com	5
cssnature.org	5

danielmillions.com	5
designflavr.com	5
digmo.org	5
directory-web.net	5
directory.classifieds1000.com	5
directoryworld.net	5
Dirjournal.com	5
dirplanet.in	5
discoverourtown.com	5
divinecss.com	5
dmegs.com	5
domaining.in	5
earthwebdirectory.com	5
elib.org	5
engineersedge.com	5
enquira.com	5
eurobreeder.com	5
exactseek.com	5
Findelio.com	5

foliofocus.com	5
frety.net	5
geniusfind.com	5
gimpsy.com	5
globallinknetworks.com	5
gmawebdirectory.com	5
goguides.org	5
healthdirectorymoz.com	5
hotel-base.com	5
html5gallery.com	5
Iillumirate.com	5
incrawler.com	5
iozoo.com	5
itravelnet.com	5
kwika.org	5
lessonplansearch.com	5
linkandthink.org	5
linksgiving.com	5
locanto.com	5

lshmentor.net	5
marketinginternetdirectory.com	5
massivelinks.com	5
mastbusiness.com	5
mastersite.com	5
mundopt.com	5
onemission.com	5
operationuplink.org	5
overlandagency.com	5
rakcha.com	5
re-quest.net	5
resourcelinks.net	5
screenalicious.com	5
screenfluent.com	5
skoobe.biz	5
splashdirectory.com	5
splut.co.uk	5
splut.com	5
submissionwebdirectory.com	5

thedesigninspiration.com	5
thetortellini.com	5
traveltourismdirectory.com	5
travelwebdir.com	5
tsection.com	5
ukdirectory.co.uk	5
uncoverthenet.com	5
usalistingdirectory.com	5
volta.net	5
w3csites.com	5
web-design-directory-uk.co.uk	5
web-dir.com	5
websitelaunchpad.com	5
webworldindex.com	5
worldsiteindex.com	5
wv-travel-directory.com	5
zepti.com	5
zorg-directory.com	5
dmegs.com	5

search4i.com	5
101besthtml5sites.com	4
1abc.org	4
247webdirectory.com	4
777media.com	4
9sites.net	4
a1webdirectory.org	4
a1weblinks.net	4
academiamexicanadecine.org	4
alistdirectory.com	4
allworldlinks.com	4
allydirectory.com	4
amidalla.de	4
ananar.com	4
anthonyparsons.com	4
authoritydirectory.com	4
awi-smi.com	4
azlisted.com	4
bestfreewebsites.net	4

bizhwy.com	4
blogannounce.info	4
blueboomerang.com	4
brownbook.net	4
buysll.com	4
charitiesdirectory.com	4
charity-charities.org	4
charity.com	4
charitylibrary.co.uk	4
charityportal.org.uk	4
chicagoix.com	4
citystar.com	4
concasida2010.org	4
congoma.org	4
craftdirectory.org/edirectory/	4
craftpop.com	4
craftsitedirectory.com	4
csscount.com	4
cyberwebsearch.com	4

deathndementia.com	4
directory.e-sangha.com	4
directory.v7n.com	4
directory4u.org	4
diroo.org	4
ebjuris.com	4
ethicaldirectory.co.uk	4
expofreightuae.com	4
fasflight.com	4
fedoma.org	4
flookie.net	4
funender.com/free_link_directory	4
gainweb.org	4
gateway-worldwide.com	4
gazingus.org	4
global-weblinks.com	4
gmdir.com	4
goongee.com	4
hedir.com	4

html5-showcase.com	4
html5mania.com	4
humanediteddirectory.net	4
icfmt.org	4
info-listings.com	4
iqnewsroom.com	4
jasminedirectory.com	4
kk-club.com	4
linkaddurl.com	4
linkcentre.com	4
linkopedia.com	4
linkpartnersdirectory.com	4
linkroo.com	4
linksnativos.com	4
linkteve.com	4
macsverige.org	4
mastermoz.com	4
moo-directory.com	4
mygreencorner.com	4

netinsert.com	4
nonar.com	4
ohs.com.au/directory/	4
onlinesociety.org	4
organiclinker.com	4
ozami.com	4
pedsters-planet.co.uk	4
phillyfirstonthefourth.com	4
prolinkdirectory.com	4
puppyurl.com	4
qango.com	4
qualityinternetdirectory.com	4
rdirectory.net	4
rightwingeye.com	4
roask.com	4
saintbarth.org	4
searchsight.com	4
seoseek.net	4
sevenseek.com	4

shobby.co.uk	4
siliconsalley.com	4
sites-plus.com	4
slackalice.com	4
spiritsearch.com	4
submitlinkurl.com	4
sundaysalonchicago.com	4
surfsafely.com	4
thalesdirectory.com	4
the-photographer-directory.com	4
tmaonline.net	4
tslindia.org	4
turnpike.net	4
txtlinks.com	4
tygo.com	4
uksuperweb.co.uk	4
unscol.org	4
viesearch.com	4
voxcap.com	4

w3catalog.com	4
web-beacon.com	4
webbozz.com	4
website-services.biz	4
websitespromotiondirectory.com	4
websquash.com	4
welovewp.com	4
wikidweb.com	4
wpbartsdistrict.com	4
wpgala.com	4
wpinspiration.com	4
wwwi.co.uk	4
yoofindit.com	4
zdirectory.net	4
askmatrix.com	4
addurl.nu	4
linkdirectory.com	4
internet-heaven.co.uk/stuff/add.php	4
9ug.com	3

alaki.net	3
allstatesusadirectory.com	3
beedirectory.com	3
bigfreeguide.com	3
bigtraveling.com	3
blogaboutmysite.com	3
candydetective.com	3
cssmania.com	3
cwrp.net	3
dearbetty.com	3
devoteclub.com	3
digitaleveuk.org	3
directmylink.com	3
directory.cnjiushang.com	3
directory.pr-club.net	3
directory.ttra2008.com	3
directory.yourartsncrafts.com	3
dirwizard.com	3
divide.org.uk	3

documentosbinarios.com	3
donation4charity.org/pages/charity-directory	3
dreamsubmitting.mylinea.com	3
eicq.org	3
eliteanswers.com/directory/	3
ewilla.com	3
fairelection.us	3
freewebsitedirectories.com	3
gii.in	3
gizmopromo.net	3
goexporters.com	3
gosearchbusiness.com	3
greenstalk.com	3
gzzt.org	3
herlight.com	3
html5elite.com	3
html5websites.net	3
hydeparkbooks.com	3
indexking.net	3

iowasilver.com	3
jaborwhalky.com	3
linknow.co.nz	3
lookforth.com	3
marketingwho.com	3
nadrealizem.com	3
netwerker.com	3
netzoning.com	3
newhealthdirectory.com	3
nkssnet.net	3
nometrix.com	3
onlineshoppers.ca	3
pmarketing.com	3
primodirectory.com	3
reallyfirst.com	3
rubberstamped.org	3
search-o-rama.com	3
searchwebworld.com	3
secondwavesystems.com	3

sitesnoop.com	3
sonoracelticfaire.co	3
speedydirectory.com	3
sudanow.net	3
thebrickwall.com/directory/	3
thegreatdirectory.org	3
ukcharities.org	3
usawebsitesdirectory.com	3
worldwidelist.net	3
wpfloat.com	3
yourjoker.com	3
directory-free.com	2
directory-global.com	2
emedinews.com/directory/	2
html-five.net	2
iwebtool.com/directory/	2
kiwidir.com	2
needaccomodation.com	2
pegasusdirectory.com	2

site-sift.com	2
webahead.net	2
websiteopening.com	2
almapubliclibrary.org	0
bigall.com	0
hitwebdirectory.com	0
directoryexpert.org	
rapidenetwork.eu	
douz.org	
webbozz.com	

Blog Directories

Domains	**PR**
technorati.com	8
alltop.com	7
blogs.com	7
globeofblogs.com	7
blogcatalog.com	6
topix.net/dir	6
blogtopsites.com	6

blogtoplist.com	6
ontoplist.com	6
hotvsnot.com	6
blogs.botw.org	6
blogarama.com	6
blogflux.com/	6
icerocket.com	6
bloggernity.com	6
blogrankings.com	6
bloghub.com	6
blogsrater.com	6
zimbio.com/company/bloggers	5
topblogarea.com	5
bloglisting.net	5
bloghints.com	5
loadedweb.com	5
webworldindex.com	5
addyourblog.com	5
crayon.net	5

blogdirs.com	5
bloggernow.com	5
bloggingfusion.com	5
placeblogger.com	5
regator.com	5
blog-directory.org/add-blog.php	5
bloguniverse.com	5
minnesota.com/blog-directory	5
blogville.us	5
nycbloggers.com	5
blog-search.com	5
buzzerhut.com	5
blogscanada.ca	5
delightfulblogs.com	5
blogtree.com	5
blogbal.com	5
bloglinker.com	5
theweblogreview.com	5
flookie.net	5

topofblogs.com	4
blogs.avivadirectory.com	4
rateitall.com/s-4679-blog-directory.aspx	4
blurtit.com	4
theseoking.com	4
fybersearch.com	4
info-listings.com	4
bloggerschoiceawards.com	4
blogio.net	4
A1weblinks.net	4
topsiteswebdirectory.com	4
blogskinny.com	4
blogadr.com	4
feedplex.com	4
feedmap.net	4
wilsdomain.com	4
blogdirectory.net	4
blogdire.com	4
blogsrating.com	4

sarthak.net	4
roask.com	4
blogsitelist.com	4
spillbean.com	4
photarium.com	4
blogpoint.com	4
spicypage.com/	4
blogsbycountry.com	4
blogdirectorysubmission.com	4
blogannounce.info	4
lazyblogdirectory.com	4
blogratings.com	4
top-blogs.org	4
wordpressblogdirectory.com	4
blogdirectory.ws	4
bloguniverse.org	4
webloogle.com	4
goblogz.com	4
blogdirectory.org.uk	4

lisblogsource.net	4
freewebs.com/blogotion	3
portal.eatonweb.com	3
lsblogs.com	3
blogs-collection.com	3
bloggeries.com	3
blogzoop.com	3
blogratedirectory.com	3
search4blogs.com/bloggers/index.php	3
blogsthatfollow.com	3
blogsforsmallbusiness.com	3
blogdir.co.uk	3
blogfolders.com	3
birminghambloggers.contactbox.co.uk	3
bloggerhq.net	3
blogshaven.com	3
websandiego.org/business/reg.php	3
blogwebdirectory.com	3
gozoof.com	3

blog.directory-seek.com	3
blogpopular.net	3
conseillemoi.net	3
bloggersdirectory.org	3
blogscollection.com	3
shoutyoursite.com	3
alotofblogs.com	3
boosterblog.net	3
aveblogs.com	3
directoryblogs.com	3
blogirific.com	3
blogpopular.com	3
wutzle.com/browse.php	3
blogsranker.com	3
liquida.com	2
bestblogs.org	2
ablogin.com	2
anse.de	2
blogvillage.gotop100.com	2

directory.bloggertalk.net	2
2searchblogs.com	2
ajdee.com/pages/Blogs/index.html	2
blogicas.com/directory	2
surrealblog.com	2
listablog.com	2
goblog4i.com	2
bloghitlist.com	2
creative-blogs.com	2
problogdirectory.com	2
blogification.com	2
themillionblogs.com	2
freeblogdirectory.info	2
blogdesam.com	2
blogsearchengine.com	1
mylot.com/w/blogs/default.aspx	1
britblog.com	1
fuelmyblog.com	1
blogdirectory.ckalari.com	1

bldir.net	1
weblogs.co.in	1
ultimateblogdirectory.com	1
pinoyblogger.com/directory	1
geoblogdirectory.com	1
heliosblogs.com/allcats.html	1
bloggercyber.com	1
bloggerinternet.com	1
exclusivedirectory.net	1
bloggerglobal.com	1
blogswirl.com	1
directories.totalblogdirectory.com	0
blog-collector.com	0
mynewblog.com/lastsites	0
blogdumps.com/index.php	0
blogit.com/blogs/default.aspx	0
blogtagstic.com	0
directory.ubdaily.com	0
splogspot.com (www.)	0

blloggs.com	0
directory.blogaz.net	0
urldigger.com	0
global-blogs.info	0
bloggazines.com	0

Article Directories

Domains	PR
TheFreeLibrary.com	7
Ezinearticles.com	6
GoArticles.com	6
SelfGrowth.com	6
Gather.com	6
ArticlesBase.com	5
ArticleDashboard.com	5
ArticleSnatch.com	5
ArticleCity.com	5
Isnare.com	5
YouSayToo.com	5
Focus.com	5

IdeaMarketers.com	4
SooperArticles.com	4
Amazines.com	4
ArticleRich.com	4
ArticleBlast.com	4
ArticleTrader.com	4
Wrytestuff.com	4
EvanCarmichael.com	4

Video Sharing

youtube.com	9
vimeo.com	9
dailymotion.com	7
metacafe.com	7
truveo.com	7
videoegg.com	7
videobomb.com	7
veoh.com	6
liveleak.com	6
ifilm.com	6

stickam.com	6
stupidvideos.com	6
blinkx.com	6
magnify.net	6
sevenload.com	6
grindtv.com	6
selfcasttv.com	6
flixya.com	5
ourmedia.org	5
mefeedia.com	5
orb.com	5
videosift.com	5
shozu.com/portal	5
pandora.tv	5
eyespot.com	5
vmix.com	5
mediamax.com	5
phanfare.com	5
clipshack.com	5

gofish.com	5
freevlog.org	5
loomia.com	5
glidedigital.com	5
vongo.com	5
vlogmap.org	5
dropshots.com	4
bigcontact.com	4
flurl.com	4
bofunk.com	4
fireant.tv	4
broadbandsports.com	4
clipmoon.com	4
gawkk.com	4
vidmax.com	4
sumo.tv	4
qoof.com	4
openvlog.com	4
podesk.com	4

popcast.com	4
tubetorial.com	3
magnoto.com	3
poddater.com	3
pixparty.com	3
grinvi.com	3
pooxi.com	3
divicast.com	3
broadsnatch.com	3
woomu.com	3
everybit.com	3
custom-niche-videos.com	2
evideoshare.com	2
boltfolio.com	2

RSS Directories

Domains	**PR**
topix.net	7
blogdigger.com	6
feedage.com	6

AFFILIATE MARKETING

feedcat.net	6
finance-investing.com	6
jordomedia.com	6
medworm.com	6
redtram.com	6
rssmountain.com	6
swoogle.umbc.edu	6
automotive-links.mustangv8.com/RSS-directory	5
chordata.info	5
gabbr.com	5
plazoo.com	5
rssmicro.com	5
rsstop10.com	5
urlfanx.com	5
5z5.com	4
educational-feeds.com	4
feedagg.com	4
feedplex.com	4
feedsee.com	4

keegy.com	4
medical-feeds.com	4
newzalert.com	4
ngoid.sourceforge.net	4
oobdoo.com	4
paiddirectory.com	4
political-humor.net	4
postami.com	4
rss-directory.us	4
rssbuffet.com	4
rssmotron.com	4
solarwarp.net	4
4guysfromrolla.aspin.com	3
anatech.net	3
moneyhighstreet.com	3
rsschomp.com	3
rssfeeds.org	3
xmeta.net	3
anse.de/rdfticker	2

Domains	
feedgy.com	2
goldenfeed.com	2
wingee.com	2
leighrss.com	1
readablog.com	1
feedlisting.com	0
millionrss.com	0
rssfeeds.com	0

Doc Sharing

Domains	PR
issuu.com	9
slideshare.net	8
scribd.com	8
docstoc.com	7
thinkfree.com	7
keepandshare.com	6
memoware.com	6
yudu.com	6
ziddu.com	6

docs.zoho.com	6
slideboom.com	6
authorstream.com	6
edocr.com	5
filefactory.com	5
uploading.com	5
wepapers.com	5
esnips.com	5
my.huddle.net	5
slideserve.com	5
pdfcast.org/pdf/	5
easy-share.com	4
gigasize.com	4
glasscubes.com	4
slingfile.com	4
slidelive.com	4
myplick.com	4
docuter.com	3
doxtop.com	3

Domains	
gazhoo.com	3
kewlshare.com	3
bookgoo.com	3
slideburner.com	3
midupload.com	2
persianupload.net	2
zshare.net	0
gotomyfiles.com	0
twidox.com	0
pex.webexone.com	0
re-pdf.com	

Press Releases

Domains	PR
businesswire.com	7
prlog.org	6
betanews.com	6
i-newswire.com	6
pitchengine.com	6
pr-inside.com	6

prlog.org	6
businessportal24.com	5
cgidir.com	5
free-press-release.com	5
information-online.com	5
live-pr.com	5
newswiretoday.com	5
openpr.com	5
prleap.com	5
przoom.com	5
pr.com	5
sbwire.com	5
pressbox.co.uk	4
afly.com	4
bignews.biz	4
businessservicesuk.com	4
clickpress.com	4
dmnnewswire.digitalmedianet.com	4
freepressindex.com	4

ideamarketers.com	4
it-analysis.com	4
it-director.com	4
onlineprnews.com	4
prfire.co.uk	4
prfree.com	4
prmac.com	4
pressbox.co.uk	4
pubarticles.com	4
theopenpress.com	4
enewswire.co.uk	4
1888pressrelease.com	4
addpr.com	3
bigrockwebdirectory.com	3
signup.ecommwire.com	3
exactrelease.com	3
express-press-release.net	3
free-press-release-center.info	3
itbsoftware.com	3

mediasyndicate.com	3
newsmakers.co.uk	3
prurgent.com	3
pr9.net	3
pressabout.com	3
pressexposure.com	3
pressmethod.com	3
prfocus.com	3
ukprwire.com	3
usprwire.com	3
postafreepressrelease.com	2
prfriend.com	2
prbd.net	2
pressreleasecirculation.com	2
releasewire.org	2
emeapr.com	1
netforcepress.com	1
astro-business.com	0
bitboot.com	0

AFFILIATE MARKETING

clickanews.com	0
clickanews.net	0
netbizresources.com	0
netforcenews.com	0
netforcepr.com	0
netforcetechnology.com	0
newsactive.net	0
newsinsites.com	0
newsphase.com	0
our-newsletter.com	0
pagerelease.com	0
pr80.com	0
pressreleasesonline.co.uk	0
seenation.com	0
tectrical.com	0
technifuture.com	0
technofrantic.com	0

www.ingramcontent.com/pod-product-compliance
Lightning Source LLC
Chambersburg PA
CBHW070655220526
45466CB00001B/453